# HOW TO GET GOD'S KIDS BACK

## Spread the Gospel, Make Disciples, and Mentor Youth in Your Local Community

## ADULTS WHO CARE

# HOW TO GET GOD'S KIDS BACK

## Spread the Gospel, Make Disciples, and Mentor Youth in Your Local Community

### ADULTS WHO CARE

## DR. NATE LANDIS

# HOW TO GET GOD'S KIDS BACK

### Spread the Gospel, Make Disciples, and Mentor Youth in Your Local Community

## ADULTS WHO CARE

### by Dr. Nate Landis



Back cover: Content derived, in part, on research compiled by the Pinetops Foundation in a report titled *The Great Opportunity* (greatopportunity.org).  Used by permission.



Publication Design & Management:  LAMP POST *publishers*

lamppostpublishers.com



Published by:

## URBAN YOUTH COLLABORATIVE

P.O. Box 124708 • San Diego • CA • 92112

www.uyc.org  ||  www.natelandis.org

Trade Paperback:  ISBN-13 # 979-8-9861195-4-0
ebook:  ISBN-13 # 979-8-9861195-5-7

**We want to be accessible to you.**

Throughout this book, we encourage you to contact us.  Please refer to the contact information below to reach us any time:

**Phone:**      **619-768-0278**

**Email:**      **courses@UYC.org**

**Website:**    **courses.UYC.org**

# ACKNOWLEDGMENTS

The kingdom work described in this book would not be possible without the tireless and dedicated efforts of the Urban Youth Collaborative (UYC) staff, student leaders, financial investors, church partners, teachers, administrators, coaches, parents, parachurch allies, and community organizations that believe in the limitless value of young people. An inspiring God-sized vision of a new city and a new version of youth ministry is too big to accomplish alone. We need the power of God and we need each other. Thank you for your friendship, sacrifice, and commitment to follow Jesus with me!

# CONTENTS

Have you ever experienced the thrill of watching someone you care about spread their wings to become all that they're meant to be?  Maybe they even had to overcome adversity or the challenges of a difficult childhood?  Would it give you satisfaction to know that, somehow, your life played a role in the success of another young person?  I think we all would love that.

I'm Dr. Nate Landis, Founder and President of Urban Youth Collaborative.  For the past twelve years, our organization has helped kids shine as lights for Christ at public schools.  It's exhilarating work when young people discover the power of Christ in them and begin shaping the destinies of their friends, teammates, and families.

No person is an island.  Young people don't thrive and discover their calling alone.  It takes a community of elders in a tribe to help the next generation unearth their true identity and life mission.

That's where you and I come in.

If you're reading this book, you're probably wondering whether you have what it takes to build a meaningful relationship with a young person. You may be asking, "Am I cool enough? Do I really have anything to offer?" I guarantee you that you have what it takes to make a lasting difference in the life of a teenager. I'll show you the way.

No matter what your past hurts or hang-ups are, there is a young person who longs for your input and presence in their lives. All you have to do is take a step of faith.

Welcome to my Adults Who Care course. I'm so excited to unpack some principles and concepts that will allow you to make a lasting impact in the life of a teenager. Regardless of where you are starting from, I know that God has a meaningful destination prepared for you. All we have to do is take the journey one step at a time.

I will guide you through the whole process. Together, we'll understand more about youth culture and how relationships with young people flourish. We'll also discover your unique gifts, talents, and experiences that give you something special to offer the next generation.

The kids God has called you to reach will benefit from the extra care, prayer, and study that you pour into this experience.

Please don't keep your struggle, your heartache, your victory, or your big dream to yourself. We're all here for you! You've joined a community of believers who are taking risks for Jesus on the front lines.

Expect adventure. Expect push-back. Expect stories of transformation. Don't ever expect to stay the same.

Are you ready?

# HOW TO GET GOD'S KIDS BACK

## Spread the Gospel, Make Disciples, and Mentor Youth in Your Local Community

### ADULTS WHO CARE

# m o d u l e   o n e

## BE YOU:  LOVE IS YOUR COLLATERAL

We're going to unlock how God can use you in the life of a young person in meaningful and eternal ways. Many people believe that relationships with youth require a magic touch, a special gift, or rare skill set only bestowed upon a select few.

I'm here to debunk that myth.

If you care enough to be reading this book, then you care enough to make a difference.  By cultivating and deploying the power of love, authenticity, and consistency in your life and relationships, you'll be on your way to a remarkable legacy of impact. Together we'll learn how.

You don't have to be an expert to guide someone else.  You only have to genuinely care about them and walk alongside their journey.  Your presence and interest will encourage them.

**Are you a few steps ahead in the adventure of life? Then you have *so much* to offer!  Period.**

3

**Are you willing to share your insights gained through your history of successes and failures?**

**Will you let a young person teach you about their world and life from a different perspective?**

If the answer is yes, then you'll accelerate growth in the life of a new young friend, and inside yourself too.

You may have experienced avoidable pitfalls that can save someone else years of agony, struggle, and heartache. You may be able to help someone keep going who's discouraged and considering throwing in the towel. You may also put someone on the fast track to significance and success because they don't have to spend a decade on trial-and-error activities. You can let someone who longs for love know that they matter, that their dreams are important, and that they are not alone in their pain!

If you take this leap of faith into the life of another young person, I guarantee that you will be blessed and learn and grow more than you could ever imagine. When we care about them from our heart, young people end up mentoring us even more than we mentor them. In many ways, youth ministry is cross-cultural. The gap between the generations can leave Boomers, Gen Xers, Millennials, and Gen Z separated by a vast chasm.

In this session we'll explore the power of three attributes that all Christians – regardless of background, life story, or education – are capable of developing because of the Holy Spirit living and at work inside us.

These three attributes are equally powerful and rare in our culture today. If you partner with God and let Him grow these traits inside your soul, you will become a stream in the desert for a lost young person trying to find their way.

The three life changing markers we're looking at today are *Love*, *Authenticity*, and *Consistency*.

*Love* and *Authenticity* make up two lanes on the bridge that can (re)connect us. Let's look at each of these two first. Then, we'll continue by focusing on the impact that takes place when we faithfully walk back and forth across that bridge with people for months, years, and decades: this is the power of *Consistency*.

## The Power of LOVE:

Love can be defined as a sincere commitment to the other's well-being. This leads to actions that benefit their long-term best interest. True selfless love is so rare in today's society that it gets attention. Everyone seems to be looking for it, yet so few seem convinced that they've found a pure form of it, let alone a love that lasts.

Jesus described love this way, "Greater love has no one than this, that someone lay down his life for his friends." (John 15:13 ESV).

Self-sacrifice without strings attached stands out in this world of reciprocal agendas where quid-pro-quo operations is usually the expected norm. Caring for another person and expecting nothing in return shocks people and creates curiosity. People have to know what's behind genuine acts of true love. Even on a small scale, these types of intentional actions go a long way.

Through the Holy Spirit, Jesus lives inside us and can teach us how to love others well. By paying attention to – I like to say *studying* – how Jesus loves us, we can gain skills when it comes to practically loving others.

As John writes, "We love because He first loved us" (1 John 4:19 ESV). If God is the source of all love, then it makes sense that we spend as much time and energy as possible discovering more about where all affection comes from. In fact, later in this same verse, God commands us to love others *because* of His great love for humanity.

So, if you're new to this idea of love being an acquired skill more than a feeling, you're not alone. Most of our culture's love songs describe love as an emotion outside of our control. It mysteriously comes and goes like a spring breeze or a passing thought.

I once attended a wedding – officiated by a life coach – where the couple gazed mistily into each other's eyes and pledged in front of their guests to "Love you for as long as love shall last." Inspiring huh? Hardly! Yet that is the style of "love" offered by our culture today.

Do you think young people are hungry for something more? You bet! They've seen a revolving door of boyfriends, girlfriends, parents, coaches, pastors, friends, leaders, and relatives who claimed to "love" them just up and leave.

Those who pass on the love of Jesus, however, look different because they love differently. The closer you draw to Jesus and experience His love for you personally, the more you'll become a conduit of that love for young people starving for it. The need for love is so strong in the human spirit that people will do anything to get it. We'll even settle for counterfeit love if the real thing is unavailable or appears to be unattainable.

I was once at a youth conference in Baltimore. At the end of the weekend, the coordinators held an open mic where young people could come up and say anything they wanted about their experience. One brave teenage girl slowly approached the microphone and, in front of several hundred of her peers, stood up and said, "I used to give guys my body if they promised to hold me for just thirty minutes afterwards." She sobbed. Her ache for love was so strong that she'd give herself away for thirty minutes of artificial affection. Yet junk food tastes pretty good when you're starving. Fortunately for the young woman in my Baltimore story, she began to open her heart up to the satisfying love and forgiveness of Christ that weekend.

We need more Christians to get skilled at loving so young people can taste the real thing.  Then they'll be less apt to get lured away by counterfeits.

If we view love as a feeling instead of a commitment to action, then we can talk ourselves out of loving certain types of people because we lack the subjective inclination in a given moment.  When we don't feel capable or lovable, we assume we couldn't possibly be worthy to receive real love or give it in a way that makes a lasting difference in the life of another.  If another person *feels* too different than us, we assume the gap is too wide for us to connect with them.

Humbly receiving the love we need from God positions us to help somebody else receive it too.  Jesus bridged the biggest relationship gap of all human history:  the gulf between sinful people and a holy God.  His work on the cross and resurrection from the dead reconciled believers back to God.  In His own body, He became the living example of a unified and reconciled God/human relationship.  When Christ lives in us and teaches us how to love, we're learning from the author of love and the world's best student – all in the same person.

If we really believe Jesus is capable of doing that, then no distance between other people is too great.  In fact, with Jesus living inside you through the Holy Spirit, His ministry of reconciliation can happen between unlikely people in ways that surprise us.  You do not have to be gifted at relationships to love well. All you need is Jesus in you.

He can speak through you . . .
He can listen through you . . .
He can serve and care through you . . .
He can love through you . . .

Jesus wants to do all of this.  Will you let Him?  He'll show you how.


## The Power of AUTHENTICITY:

I'm a white, half-deaf, 44-year-old who grew up in the midwest. Now I joyfully live and serve youth and families in the inner-city of San Diego.  I'm often the minority at community schools and certain churches I partner with.  What makes me effective?  My collateral in cross-cultural relationships is *authenticity*.

At first, I tried guessing what others wanted me to be like and I tried to become that.  Back in my college days, I remember developing a Puerto Rican accent because I wanted to fit in with the church crowd I ran with in North Philadelphia.  Some people think reaching someone else requires us to change in order to be like them.  I used to believe that too.  I changed the way I talked, dressed, walked, and carried myself hoping this would make me more attractive and effective in certain communities.

The relationship approach we're discussing here is about Christ in you.  Humans look on the outward appearance.  It's God who sees the heart of a person (1 Samuel 16:7).  Therefore, you do not need to pretend to be someone you're not in order to reach others (in this case youth).

I used to think I am too ________________ to make a difference with kids – particularly young people from an urban background different from my own upbringing.

- White

- Deaf (my right ear was dead from birth; my left ear is 80% good)

- Privileged (compared to many)

- Old (in the eyes of some)

What goes into your "blank" when you think about the idea of making a difference in a young person's life?

Take a quiet and honest moment with yourself. What would you insert in your blank? Here's a promising proposition. What if, instead of something that disqualifies you or renders you useless, our weaknesses and brokenness can actually be a gift that forces Christ to shine out of our cracks?

The gift of having to rely on God rather than your own "juice," draw, appeal, etc., makes you more powerful precisely *because* you can't fool yourself into thinking you're enough on your own. In this humble posture, we're not tempted to trade the power of God's Spirit for our own ability to connect. We know the Holy Spirit – Christ in us – makes it possible to connect with the true essence of another's soul.

People who rely on their own skill may be able to close a deal. People who rely on the Holy Spirit's empowerment can close on destiny.

Kids have strong *authenticity* detectors – especially those who have been hurt before. They keep me honest. That's why I love working with them. As the light of Christ shines through our cracks, the warmth and brightness will draw young people to Christ in you. As we open ourselves to God and others, those relationships teach us to see the world from the perspective of another. We may be surprised by what we find.

An authentic desire to know God and others as they really are frees us to receive whatever He has for us. Authenticity requires us to let go of preconceived ideas about God and others who may be different than us.  Studying the scriptures and genuinely seeking God's will can be exhilarated when two different people find unity at the foot of the cross.

**That's the adventure available to those who dare to embrace God's call to authentic relationships across the generations!**

There is a hunger in all of us that God wants to fulfill.  When we remove pretense and posturing, we can discover this together.  Yet we cannot pass out what we do not have.  We can only reproduce what we are.

As we authentically grow closer to God and get healthier ourselves, we have much to offer the coming generation as we walk with them.  There is a quality of life and relationships only possible through Christ.  Taste and see that God's plans are good.

## The Power of CONSISTENCY:

In addition to authenticity, kids who have been let down before also look for *consistency*.  Whether they know it or not, it's a measure they use to size others up.  When mom's boyfriend keeps changing, young people learn not to grow too attached.  When principals and youth pastors come and go, kids learn to survive by lowering expectations.  They'd rather stay lonely than get hurt worse.  When coaches and family members bail, kids play it off like they don't care much anymore.  A protective numbness of heart is the first sign of despair.  By staying consistent, God's people provide hope.

When kids *can see* God's people behaving consistently in relationships, it makes it easier to believe in *the unseen* God we represent.  Showing up and staying involved are two of your biggest moves.  Mastering them will set us apart.  Sadly, something so simple has become rare.  Relish the simplicity of not running away, giving in, or giving up.

Yes, it will get hard.  Nothing worth doing is ever easy.  As foster parents, my wife and I take in kids who need a loving and stable home while their parents figure life out.  The cardinal rule of the experience is that we are not allowed to give them back until the court decides where their forever home will be.  No matter how hard it gets, we can never throw in the towel until our place-ment finishes.  Believe me, there were days when I wondered if we could make it.  Raising adorable babies recovering from meth and neglect brings unique challenges.  One thing my wife and I committed to was never giving them back until the journey is complete.  We've had two successful placements – of three siblings each – where our consistency allowed the family to reunite.  A happy ending!

As Christians, consistency provides stability and hope for chil-dren and adolescents we care for.  We model what God's faithful-ness looks like for those who are unsure it exists.  This practice, in turn, teaches kids to be faithful in their significant relationships too.  In their impressionable young brains, the idea of family and quality human connections seems possible.

Love, bonding, and attachment takes place because of our con-sistency.  This gives them the courage and context to form mean-ingful relationships with others along the path of life.  The ability to bond in early childhood and adolescence gives children an emo-tional and relational lifeline for future relationships with friends, employers, professors, relatives, a significant other, and society as a whole.  Without this gift of healthy bonding, young people grow up unable to attach and experience the quality relationships their souls were designed to crave.

Relationships are the lifeblood of humans. Your consistency tells a young person whether hope for personal connection is worth holding onto or not.

The video version of this course contains some additional questions designed to help you share your life experience with a young person. You can find these online at courses.uyc.org/adults-who-care. As you consider these, block off some time to get alone with yourself and God. Honestly and diligently work through these. It will be well worth it. I am convinced that you can make a difference that lasts – in this life and the life to come! Stretching yourself to be used by God in the life of a young person will bless you too.

Thanks for being you and thanks for being available.

In the next module, we'll unpack how your unique story and experience can be a blessing in the life of a young person hungry for connection and direction.

# module two

## YOU CARRY SOMETHING VALUABLE

Through each new module, we get to explore the deeper recesses of how God has wired us for relationships. In the last module, we considered the transforming power of love, authenticity, and consistency in our relationships. In this module, I want to reflect on the fact that – know it or not, believe it or not, appraise it right or not – you carry something valuable. We'll do some soul excavating to discover what God has put in there.

As stewards, our task is to do the hard work of digging, discovering, and developing the buried treasures God placed in *you* to bless the world with. *God's gifts to us are not only for our own enjoyment nor just for our immediate family. They are put there to benefit the world. Others* – that's the name of the kingdom game! Our job is to partner with God to get them *out* so they can benefit a world that desperately needs them. That's right . . . The world desperately needs *you*! That's why God made someone so unique and special.

Not only will we be accountable for digging, discovering, and developing our treasure, we are responsible to *get it out to the world.*

Ephesians 2:8-10:

> [8] For by grace you have been saved through faith . . . it is the gift of God; [9] not as a result of works, so that no one may boast (NASB). [10] For we are his workmanship, created in Christ Jesus for good works, which God prepared ahead of time for us to do (CSB).

**Do you believe you have an assignment (a kingdom job to do) that's bigger than your trade?** That's what we have the privilege of exploring during our time together!

Those of you who are familiar with leadership language probably have come across the phrase, "We don't know what we don't know." This statement refers to the reality that humans cannot possibly be aware of all the knowledge available within a certain field of study. In fact, it takes a certain amount of intellectual work to begin understanding how much we do *not* know.

This realization can be both humbling and awe inspiring. The more astronomers study the vastness of the universe, for example, they become more aware – some would say awestruck – at how *big* the cosmos is. The further they go, the more they discover how much there still is to learn. You'll never hear any astronomer worth their salt say, "Yup, I've pretty much mastered the universe. I personally have a handle on all there is out there."

God is the same way. As the grand designer of the universe, he's even bigger than we could ever imagine. That's why he's going to give us all of eternity to discover more and more about Him. The more we study, the more we know there is to know.

When I completed my Master of Divinity degree, I felt awkward because I now had a large parchment on my wall stating that I, Nate Landis, was somehow a "Master of Divinity" after only four years of hard work. One of my colleagues at Gordon-Conwell Theological Seminary suggested that our degrees should read, "Mastered by Divinity" instead. That's getting closer. But also refers to a process that takes far longer than four years.

Think about this. We'll learn new things about God and see deeper into His ways and character forever without running out of more discoveries. *Amazing*! We all get to go on a long winding journey to discover more about God. *We get to lock in our progress* of knowing Him deeper, beginning now and continuing on throughout the unending ages.

Not only do good leaders dedicate themselves to knowing God more fully, they also devote considerable time, effort, and resources to understanding themselves better. By studying the art, you learn more about the master artist and what he intended by making the masterpiece.

While it is impossible to know all of what we do know, it is equally possible to not know what we *already do* know. What in the world do I mean by that? That's the fun part that we are going to run hard after in this module!

Over the course of our lives, we have all been blessed to acquire gifts, skills, knowledge, experience, and wisdom that we use every day without realizing the full extent of what we know. We are now so familiar with it, it has become *second nature* to us. We swim in the waters, we use skills, knowledge, and truths so much each day that we do not realize how much background we draw upon to do what we do. What is mundane and obvious to one person is a searing life-changing insight for another.

I want to encourage you today with this reality.

You carry something valuable and use it skillfully every day. Yet you may not realize how special and rare it is because it is so common in your world. You carry something that you use every day that someone else will benefit from. Don't write yourself off as a gift to another person simply because you don't realize how important your everyday skill set could be to another.

The enemy doesn't just want your soul, he wants your dreams too. If he gets your soul, he only has you. If he can capture, kill, or divert your God-given dreams, then he has destroyed your ability to impact the world for Jesus. The unique qualities you possess may seem simple to you, yet they are rare for many young people who need someone just like you in their lives.

If you would like to explore your own personality makeup, there are many sources available for mapping this out. You can take a Strength Finders inventory (DISC Profile). There is the Myers-Briggs Type Indicator. Lately the Enneagram Personality Test has become popular in leadership and ministry circles. Regardless of what assessment tool you choose to examine yourself with, I want to encourage you to spend extra time in scripture with a trusted believer who can help you exegete yourself in light of God's word. Test everything by God's word and hold fast to what is good (1 Thessalonians 5:21). You cannot help a young person on their journey toward self-understanding unless you are exploring the contours of your own heart too.

Mentoring and discipleship has become a lost art. We should always have someone pouring into us as we pour our lives into another. No matter what level of life you get to, this principle remains true. God intends us to be in disciple-making relationships with someone "above" us and someone under our wing. I use the word "above" in quotes because Christ-centered mentoring is always a two-way street where God shapes us through the relationship in equal amounts, if not more.

We can only give out what we have. We reproduce whatever we are. We must keep on growing to have something to give. We must keep on giving in order to keep growing.

As we discover our identity in Christ, then we can help coach others to walk in their true identity also. Similarly, we cannot care for youth if we do not care for ourselves too. Jesus commanded us to love others as we love ourselves. I believe He was giving us a commandment while also making an observation: We will love others in the same way that we love ourselves. If we do not fully receive and revel in the acceptance that Christ has for us, there is no way we will be able to share that freely and transparently with others. Once we get familiar with this, we become conduits that allow God's love to flow through us into the lives of others.

Geologists tell us that the Dead Sea is dead because it does not have any water flowing out of it. By not giving anything away (only conserving) the sea dies. Our lives are the same way. If we try to save our life, Jesus says, we'll lose it (Matthew 16:25). The tighter we squeeze, the more it will slip right through our fingers. But if we give away our lives for Him and the gospel, we will truly find life . . . to the fullest!

That is the kingdom riddle. Save yourself, your church, your organization, your business, and you'll likely lose it. Or at least its most significant expression of kingdom impact. On the other hand, if we give it away, surrendering it for the gospel and Christ's work, you'll find it.

Again, in the video course, you will find some introspective questions about what shapes our understanding of ourselves (what we have to offer) and what our own relationship with God is like. With each of these exercises, I really want to encourage you to carve out some focus time – at least twenty to thirty minutes – to do some real soul searching in God's presence.

I want to challenge you to invite another trusted Christian friend along on this journey. Let them know what you're considering. Invite them to pray with you. Ask them to be a conversation partner as you explore God's will for your life.  You'll be glad you did.

In the next module, I'm going to share more about how to find life by giving yours away.  It's counterintuitive.  That's exactly how Jesus loves to work in our lives.  We'll tackle the tough question of how to invest in things that really last, now and forever.

# module three

## DO WHAT LASTS:
## INVEST YOURSELF WISELY

In our previous discussion, we talked about the treasure you're carrying inside that was put there for others. We did some hard excavation work and shared the struggle of appraising the treasure properly to get it *out* so it can bless others. Now that we've done the hard work of getting to that treasure, now we're going to look at how to *invest* it. I'm going to challenge you to find places to put it where it can *multiply* and make a *lasting impact,* now and forever.

On judgment day, we all will answer to God for our life stewardship. All humans stand before the great white throne. This is the "heaven or hell" judgment. It's one nobody can afford to get wrong. That's why I'm an evangelist who has dedicated his life to making sure people have an opportunity to hear and experience the good news about Jesus.

There is a second judgment, too, that does not get as much attention. It is the bema seat where Christ will reward His followers for what they did in this body during our life on earth. Everything we did for Christ that lasts will result in reward. Whatever burns up and disappears will cause us to suffer loss. Jesus promises to wipe every tear from the eyes of believers. My goal in life is to cry more tears of joy on judgment day and few tears of regret.

As I sit here writing this, COVID-19 has taken its toll on the economy and ravaged businesses. The stock market plunged a staggering 37% off its peak at the beginning of the year. People have seen vast amounts of wealth wiped out in just a few short weeks. What if that was all we had to live for? It is humbling to admit that a person can work hard their whole life only to see everything they own decimated.

Jesus wisely told us not to store up treasure on earth where moths and rust (and bear markets) destroy. But store up treasure in heaven where thieves do not break in and steal. For where your treasure is, there your heart will be also (Luke 12:33-34). Like a magnet to metal, the human heart automatically follows wherever we have placed our treasure. According to Jesus, it is entirely possible to invest your life's resources where it can painfully disappear. Anyone who stores up treasures on earth without doing so in heaven, will be brutally disappointed on judgment day. We can climb the ladder of success only to realize it is leaning against the wrong building.

This is the time when I get to have a heart-to-heart moment with you to ask these questions: What are you really living for? What matters most to you? What does God have to say about your life trajectory? Will you be disappointed or elated on judgment based on how you're spending your life now? The good news is it is not too late to change. If you've made it this far in the book, God probably has been gripping your heart and challenging you to invest your life where it can get the greatly lasting reward. We owe it to God, ourselves, our families, and those God called us to reach to think this way. Life is short. The Bible describes it as a vapor and a breath. When you and I stand in front of Christ to give an account for everything, what will He say about us?

Let me submit to you that there is not a more valuable place to invest your time, talents, and treasure than into the lives of the next generation. Anything we do for Christ is stored up forever into eternity. We do not earn our salvation or a place in heaven. This only happens by grace through faith in the perfect work of Jesus Christ through His death and resurrection. Yet we do earn rewards based on how we spend our lives. The greatest reward of all is being with Christ forever and those who know Him because of our lives on earth.

As you master the relationship arts of loving, authenticity, and consistency, you'll likely be fortunate enough to enjoy the fruits of ministry on this side of eternity too. Nothing is more rewarding, now and forever. If you're breathing air, it's never too late to get started.

After one of my sermons, a 78-year-old woman came up to me and said, "God called me to start a prison ministry two years ago. Everyone is about half my age and has more tattoos than me." She went on to tell me that at age 76, she started doing Bible studies in prison and inviting inmates to find freedom in Jesus Christ. Pretty exciting! Moses got his call and kingdom assignment at age 80. Does that give any late bloomers hope? It should. Availability is much more important to God than age.

How much of ourselves, our lives, our time, our finances are we willing to give to Him? That is the bigger question. The conversation shifts dynamically when we realize that everything we have is on loan from God to begin with[1]. We don't own ourselves, our

---

1    Kenneth H. Blanchard and Phil Hodges, *The Servant Leader: Transforming Your Heart, Head, Hands, & Habits* (Nashville, TN: J. Countryman, 2003).

spouses, our time, our jobs, our money, our property, our church, our business, our stocks, or our kids. From a New Testament perspective, it all belongs to God in the first place. There is no "ours" or "mine" if we think biblically.

We are all stewards of what God has entrusted to us. He'll be returning one day to settle accounts with his servants. The question will be, "What did you do with what you were given?" Those who multiply what they received, receive a greater reward. Those who hid what they had because they were afraid, lose everything and are thrown into "outer darkness" where there will be "weeping and gnashing of teeth" (Matthew 25:30). Yikes!

I'm not trying to guilt you or scare you into doing youth ministry. I do, however, want you to take the words of Jesus seriously and find that mission – whatever it is – that he has put you on earth to accomplish. If it is some type of engagement with you – great! I'd be delighted to keep our conversation going. If God calls you to another kingdom assignment – do it with all your heart. The important thing is that you find it and go after it fully!

My "thing" is evangelism and Christian community development. I sense a particular call to do this among youth and families in an urban context. That's me. What's your kingdom thing or special assignment? Let's find out! Now is a wonderful time to get started. There is no time to waste. We need to learn – as Professor Haddon Robinson taught me – to count our days so that our days will count.

When I got ordained, one of my friends from the black Pentecostal tradition closed out the service. He gave me a life challenge that I want to share with you here: "The most valuable land on earth," he told me and those in attendance, "is not oil fields in the Middle East, diamond mines in Africa, or a gated community in Rancho Santa Fe. The most valuable land on earth is the cemeteries. That's where all the dreams that never got out from people's lives lie trapped for all eternity. There's a cure for cancer," he said, "buried somewhere in a cemetery. It did not get out because a 7th grader got made fun of in science class because he was smarter than the other kids. Instead of developing his dream he let it die. He traded it to become popular. There's a cure for our social divisions," he went on, "but it is six feet under the earth because the person carrying it waited too long to find it and use it. She kept saying 'Once my kids get a little older, once we have more money, once my husband gets through this difficult season in our marriage.'

"Once upon a time became no time. Someone walked around on earth with a grand idea that would allow the age-old gospel to get preached faithfully to a new generation, but it stayed locked inside because the person was afraid of criticism, so they kept it hidden. Now it lies hidden for all time. In the cemetery. When you're done with your ministry," my dear friend told me, "make sure you *die empty!*"

Whatever God put inside you, get it all out. Every last drop. All the pieces. Then put them together and use what's inside for the good of humanity, for our world, and for the gospel! It belongs to Christ. You owe it to him to put it to use. Count your days so your days will count. And, by all means, die empty!

I preached a sermon like that at a church one Sunday. A woman came up to me afterwards and said, "I've got a book in me. It will help people get closer to God. I need to get it out." I like that. What's inside you that needs to get out?

In the video course at courses.uyc.org/adults-who-care, take some time to consider the development questions about your deepest passions. Where the world's deepest needs align with your strongest passions, at that point you may just find God's will for your life.  As you dive into these, allow yourself time to pray, study scriptures, and let this exercise sink in.

You'll be glad you did.  The people you touch through your life will be glad too!

In the next module, we're going to take a look at the heart and soul of Generation Z, our nation's elementary, middle, and high school students.  Understanding them better will help us love and reach this generation that Jesus cares so much about.  Thanks for loving them too!

# module four

## A GENERATION AT A CROSSROADS: YOUR TIME IN HISTORY

We've considered the importance of investing our lives wisely by understanding our God-given assignment and spending ourselves in places that last and maximize our impact. Now we're going to dive a little deeper into the cultural waters to understand our time in history and what contemporary students are going through. Then we'll try to discern what God may be saying to the church. "How then," asked Francis Shaeffer, "ought we to live?"

Generation Z (our nation's current elementary, middle, and high school students) is the largest generation in US history, and as of 2020 they comprise over twenty percent of the United States population. Yet *one million* youth per year are exiting churches because they do not see faith – or at least institutional religion – as relevant to their lives. According to Fuller Youth Institute, in order for a young person to "stick" and stay in church into adulthood, they need meaningful relationships in their lives with *at least three adults other than the youth pastor* during adolescence. These people

25

fill the vital role of showing someone what it looks like to follow Christ in the decades after high school.[2] Youth need adults who are wholehearted in their devotion to Christ. These genuine disciples make Christian living look attractive.

One ethicist I read defined a saint as someone who makes it a little easier to believe in God. Each generation of saints, then, collectively needs to make it a little easier for those coming after them to embrace Christian faith and life in the local church. Unfortunately, each US generation, as we move from Boomers, to Xers, to Millennials, and on to Generation Z, has seen significant declines in believers who come after them. According to the Barna Group, the "pattern is indisputable: The younger the generation, the more post-Christian it is."

As we discussed earlier, honing our skills when it comes to love, authenticity, and consistency will go a long way to ensuring that more young people embrace faith in Christ. This relational skill set will work no matter what generation we find ourselves in. Fuller's insight about a community of faith puts the burden on all members of a congregation and generation to successfully pass the baton of Christianity on to the next generation. Each society is only one generation away from Christianity going extinct.

This approach to youth ministry is not a recipe for "outsourcing" the spiritual growth of teenagers to the youth pastor and a few college volunteers alone. When the youth group is seen as the toy department of church affairs, kids grow up without the support they deserve and lack experience in the broader intergenerational fellowship of believers. It takes a household of faith – an entire congregation of contagious adult disciples – in order to see a lasting and vibrant Christian get spirituality passed on to Generation Z.

---

2    fulleryouthinstitute.org/blog/what-makes-faith-stick-during-college

You could be part of mentoring relationships that anchor a kid's life and bonds them to lifelong faith in Christ.

Adults have the power to sway young people who otherwise default to the cultural norm of fleeing the faith or viewing it as something you graduate from upon leaving high school.  In fact, it is hard to take kids past where their parents are when it comes to Christian maturity.  There are glorious exceptions to what I am saying, but generally speaking, it often holds true once kids reach their twenties and beyond.

Even though the media, friends, school, and parents are powerful influences in the lives of adolescents, it is *interesting to note that Fuller's study claims adult role models play the deciding role in whether a kid stays in the faith past high school.*

A parent's worldview and value system are often what charts the course for kids.  What matters most for parents gets *caught* even more than *taught.*  Your relationship with a teenager could cause a young person to stay involved in faith or toss it aside when they get "serious" about "real life."  What a legacy!  The time you spend with a young person may not seem that significant, but it is revolutionary when you chart out the course of their lives.

Think with me for a second about a compass.  In navigation, there is a principle called the "1 in 60 rule."  For every 1 degree you are off course, you miss your target destination by 1 mile for every 60 miles you travel.  Being off by just a few degrees makes a huge difference.  Walk like that for a few hours and you can end up a few miles off course.  Travel for a week and you end up in the wrong state.  Travel for months and you end up in the wrong country.  Wow!  If you can alter the direction of a young person's life by just a few degrees during middle school or high school, they end up in a different life and a different eternal country.

Helping a young person with "life orienteering" is what this call is all about.  Most young people are not fortunate enough to have someone come alongside them to coach them and help them make important adjustments. Many wander through life with no compass. Others were handed a compass, but it's broken and leads away from the promised land.

One recent Southern California study found that families spend only thirty-seven minutes of quality time together each weekday.[3] Even though our society is busier than ever before, we are all starved for love and attention. Pastor Rick Warren writes that, "Love is spelled T-I-M-E."[4] Given the stats we just looked at, how much L-O-V-E is the current generation feeling from adults?

Perhaps the COVID-19 "pause" is giving families and loved ones an opportunity to reconnect and reprioritize as we wait for society to gradually reopen. And when it does reopen, there is an open question: How will a new generation of young people ever hear about Jesus, much less be motivated to embrace His call to discipleship?

The US Department of Health and Human Services reports that the average US teen spends two minutes per day on "religious activities!" Now, more than ever, young people need caring adults to show them the way to life in Christ.

Consider this idea. What if the role models who spend the most time with kids, earn the right to influence them? In my neighborhood, gangs fill the void left when families and social structures fracture. By becoming a substitute family, gangs "earn the right" to influence young and vulnerable kids. This same dynamic allows coaches to become substitute fathers on the football team. Or an art mentor to show a young girl how to express herself on a canvas. Young men and women are wired to be influenced by village elders

---

3    www.studyfinds.org/american-families-spend-37-minutes-quality-time
4    Warren, Rick. *The Purpose Driven Life: What on Earth Am I Here For?* Grand Rapids, MI: Zondervan, 2007.

who can sway them *toward* God or *away* from Him.  At this time in history, the direction of this new generation matters more than ever.

According to new research, we are at a tipping point in US history.  Depending on which way our compass points, our nation will end up as a predominately post-Christian society or experience another Great Awakening.  Based on current trends, I cannot imagine very much in between those two options.

Generation Z gives us a picture of the future if nothing changes.  "The most defining characteristic of Generation Z," notes James Emery White, "is that it is arguably the first generation in the West (certainly in the United States) that will have been raised in a post-Christian context."[5]  If you are someone who believes young people still need Jesus and good, godly role models, this is the ministry for you.

In your mind's eye, paint a picture of a teenager growing up as a "none," which, by the way, is the largest and fastest growing religious affiliation in the country.

I'm not talking about devout, celibate Catholics with habits and frocks, I'm talking about the rising group of young Millennials who claim "no religious affiliation whatsoever" or "none" on social science surveys.  36% percent of young Millennials fall into this rapidly growing category.  In the US right now, there are four former Christians for every new convert to Christ.

Next, imagine what a generation will be like if the vast majority do not live out Christian faith in a tangible or direct way.  Finally, envision a country where people do not have a moral compass or a value system to guide their thoughts and actions.  That's where we are heading, and the pace has accelerated in the past decade.

---

5    White, James Emery. *Meet Generation Z: Understanding and Reaching the New Post-Christian World.* Grand Rapids, MI: Baker Books, 2017.

But now is not the time for despair.  Rather it is a time for prayer and action.  With every crisis comes great opportunity for God to move in our lives in fresh ways.  My job, and the job of others like me, is to issue a clarion call to rally the church, both individually and collectively, to band together and go after a lost generation, and teach them to be a generation that Jesus loves passionately.  Their potential and value are too great to ignore.

Generation Z represents a strategic crop of America's young people upon which the future hinges.  I believe this moment and history will allow the church to awaken and shine.  We have the privilege of being part of the adventure.  As an unlikely and imperfect band of brothers and sisters, God has chosen us to be His hands and feet to live out Christ's kingdom and join with Him to get His kids back again.  Keep reading, and we'll look at some practical ideas for getting involved.

module five

# YOU'RE NEEDED: STRETCHING TO BRIDGE THE DIVIDE

We find ourselves at a critical juncture in our nation's history. We are literally losing a generation. This is the time for the church, for people of faith and goodwill, to rise and make a difference for Jesus. Our lives are short. The need is real. The window of opportunity is closing a little every day. Never has there been a time in history when a concentrated investment in a generation can be more pivotal for the nation and world. Young people matter too much to Jesus. Our call from God is clear.

Your investment in the following areas will have a multiplied and eternal return in the life of a young person – and perhaps exponentially upon an entire generation. Find some good soil to plant your:

*Time* – Whether you wear a Rolex or a Timex, we all get the same 1,440 minutes each day. Time lost can never be regained. As Rick Warren says, "We can always make

31

more money, we can never make more time.  Invest (not just "spend" or "kill" it) wisely.

***Talent*** – Your unique abilities, experiences, skills, knowledge, abilities, make up, and of course, spiritual gifts. You know what you know, and you know what you don't know.  It's all inside, put there by God for a big purpose. It all goes into who you are!

***Treasure*** – Your relationships, associations, financial resources, property, assets, tools, and opportunities that you can share with others as a wise investment.

None of us get to hold onto any of these T's after they pass through our care.  They're not ours to keep.  We can't hold onto them for long even if we try.  So, we might as well use them in ways that gain eternal outcomes.  As the missionary Jim Elliot said so well, "He is no fool who gives what he cannot keep to gain what he cannot lose."  As we have previously discussed, everything we have belongs to God already.  We might as well put it to work in ways that please Him and represent His interests.

There is a God-sized kingdom dream specific to *your* life that I want to discover with you.  Whether we know it or not, like it or not, or even believe it, *all* our time, talent, and treasure is already going *somewhere.*  We are spending all we have to fulfill the dream of a boss, a family member, a friend, society at large, or someone else's expectations of us.  Or perhaps we are just trying to survive another day and eke out an existence.  The only question is this: are you putting it into a place that lasts forever, or somewhere that will evaporate on judgment day?

There is a reason why people weep and gnash their teeth. They see what their lives *could* have been but now is no longer possible. They also see their future apart from God's presence and all the relationships they care about.

## The Value of Growing Older

One of the encouraging things about getting older (yes, there are several) is that the power of your T's usually increases over time. Think about it. While testosterone (t) levels naturally fall off over time, and other T-cells are rumored to be reduced with age, the T's on our list grow as you get older, especially as you approach your silver years. Free time can become more abundant as you experience career success, leverage, delegation, and perhaps (semi) retirement. Talents have potential to amass through a lifetime of training, development, practice, study, diverse experiences, cultivation, and wise stewardship. Treasure can grow and multiply over the years through wise stewardship. It is not meant to be hoarded but rather sent ahead to eternity through faithful kingdom investments on earth. The realization that our "T-power" grows over time should encourage us all!

The truth is you have *much* to offer the next generation. In turn, they have much to share with you too. My significance and yours is not found in earning capacity but rather *yearning* capacity. This happens when we passionately follow the plan that Christ has for our lives. As the Apostle Paul wrote to the Philippians, "Brothers, I do not consider that I have made it my own. But one thing I do: forgetting what lies behind and straining forward to what lies ahead, I press on toward the goal for the prize of the upward call of God in Christ Jesus" (Philippians 3:13 ESV).

## The Value of Staying Young at Heart

Bob Shank, founder of The Master's Program, says, "You only grow old when your memories start meaning more to you than your dreams." Will you be defined by your past or a dynamic future God's calling you to? Whether good memories we treasure and long to relive or searing regrets we long to erase, our past can anchor our consciousness and prevent us from following Jesus into the new land He wants to show us.

No matter our chronological age, we're all babies in light of eternity's timetable. God wants us to come to Him like little children who:

- Relish time with Him and cannot get enough. "Do it again!"

- Trust all that they are to their heavenly dad.

- Expect to go on adventures together!

- Are willing to *change* and *humbly* approach God like little children (for Jesus says we *cannot* enter the kingdom of heaven unless we do).

- Allow kids to become our mentors who teach us how to embrace child-like faith that pleases God.

## Your Life Legacy:

If you're like me, sometimes you might feel like you don't have that much to offer to God. Yet one of God's most powerful questions throughout scripture is, "What is in your hand?"

The angel of the Lord asked Moses, "What is in your hand?" (Exodus 4:2).

Elisha asked the widow, "What do you have in the house?" (2 Kings 4:2).

Jesus asked his disciples, "How many loaves do you have? Go and see" (Mark 6:38).

In all three examples:

The person gave what they had – all of it – to God in faith.

They obeyed with anticipation.

God transformed what they had, multiplied it, and gave it back to them to bless others.

Right now, let's start by finding whatever you have in your hand, in your house, or in your group of close associates. That's where we all start. We give it to God in faith. Letting go is hard. Opening our hands teaches us that all we have comes from God in the first place.

It is also impossible to keep something intended for others to enjoy without destroying it. Think of a butterfly that you were blessed to have land in your hand. If you close your hand to keep it from escaping, you actually destroy the life and beauty you were hoping to preserve. When we learn to let go, then we *trust* God enough to give what matters most to him.

It might not seem like much, but it is all we have. God honors the sacrifice as an act of faith. He then takes what we gave, changes it, and gives it back to us in a form that is more useful.  Often this is for a bigger purpose than we could ever envision the thing being used for:

- A shepherd's staff leads millions to freedom from the most powerful empire on earth.

- A jar of oil changes a family forever:  economic slavery to security.

- A boy's lunch feeds 15,000-20,000 with leftovers!

Never underestimate what God can do with small things we surrender to Him.  He starts with the raw material already found in our lives.  He creates and recreates using what is in and around us.

***The biggest mistake the characters in these stories could make is not giving what they had to God.***  As characters in our own stories, the biggest mistake we can make is not doing the same because:

- We may not want to part with what we have.

- We may not think what we have is worth much at all.

- We may not believe God is big enough to make our small offering into anything significant.

I want you to do an exercise with me right now.  I am going to invite you to courageously and symbolically stretch out your hand.  It represents whatever we're carrying (regrets, fears, dreams, sin, skills, abilities, every part of your story).  As you open your hand to God, he begins to work. He'll never take something away that is not eventually replaced with something better. He gets to define why and how something is "better." Can you trust him? You may even find that he returns what you gave back to you in a transformed state.

## Walking By Faith:

Avoid a life of unused legacy by engaging in these practical ideas:

1. If you are also reviewing the video course at courses.uyc.org/adults-who-care, review this module's questions and spend some time reflecting on what you've already been given.

2. Then courageously ask yourself if you'll surrender it to God.

3. If you only have God (no dream, no mission, no other job), would God be enough? This is the true act of surrender.

4. Be ready for God to surprise you!

## Dream Big:

"What do you have? Go see." – Jesus (Mark 6:38)

Who do you know that could journey with you as you discover God's plan for your life? Is there someone who could affirm and help expand your passion for young people?

What are you most passionate about?

What in life gives you a holy frustration? What needs to change because it is not the way it ought to be?

Where does the world's greatest need intersect with your biggest passion? That "sweet spot" may just be God's will for your life.

What skills and abilities matter most to you? Would you be willing to pass them along to the next generation? If so, how?

What would you do if money was no barrier? What financial resources do you already have? Where could you put it to use?

Did you take time and give your all to explore those questions? If so, good! Tuck those away in your head, in your heart, and in your notes. We'll be returning to these throughout the rest of our time together.

Finally, I'd like to conclude this module by looking at some practical ways you can escape the bubble and expand your circle of influence with kids.

## Where Will Your Feet Take You?

In order for people to benefit from what God puts in your hand, our feet need to carry us to the people in need. Often, we do not walk to all the places we could to meet the people God wants to introduce us to. This happens for many reasons. Happily, the barriers that keep us from stepping out further in faith can be overcome. Barriers may be in our minds or actual structures. Either way, walking by faith can take us farther than we ever imagined before.

Here are a few exercises that can help expand your circle of influence with kids. Feel free to try a few of these on for size to see what fits.

## Expanding Your Circle of Influence with Kids:

**Host a shadow day for a young person on your job.** Your "ordinary" job or occupation may be of "extraordinary" interest to a student interested in the same profession. Invite them to "be you" and fly as your wingman for a day.

**Invest financially in a youth-focused organization.** Your gift could help a ministry or non-profit multiply their impact in the community. It will likely touch many lives and give you an opportunity to make a lasting difference in the lives of the next generation.

**Mentor a leader of a youth-focused organization** who might benefit from your business savvy expertise, life experience, or gifts in a particular field. Relationships like this end up being two-way streets that expand our minds, hearts, and worldviews to receive from others different than ourselves.

**Serve on the board of a youth-focused organization.** Your wisdom and vision can help them achieve their God-given goals. They may be looking for someone just like you.

**You don't have to go it alone** when it comes to finding a place to connect either. Let UYC or other trusted networks of ministries help you find your place in the world of youth work. Stay connected and ask us to walk with you. We'll talk about how soon!

**Realize your social location no longer needs to limit the sphere of youth** who Christ may want to introduce you to. Jesus is a boundary crossing God. He loves to transgress the social barriers humans have erected to show how powerful God's reconciling work can be. In Christ, we have more in common than we have to divide us.

**Is there a "gatekeeper" you can meet** with that knows the world of youth and minister to them? If so, start there by taking them out for coffee or visit them in action.

**Where is the "road from Jerusalem to Jericho" in your community?** That's the place people dare not walk because it is dangerous and unknown. Do you dare to go there if God calls you to? He's the good shepherd who calms our fears as we walk with Him through the valley of the shadow of death.

Of all the fears out there, I hope the one that gets the lion's share of our attention is: "What would the world be like if we neglect the dream God has given us?" Every kid who dies on the street, goes to bed hungry, has no one to tutor them, must endure a broken family, who does not hear about Jesus, has no arena to develop their gifts, or lives in oppressive or broken environments is the consequence of someone *not* following a dream that involved that person.

The world is waiting for you to unpack and live out your God-given dream. Are you ready? I want to help you reach them.

In the next module we will move closer to our goal. We will examine the core changes we can make in our lives in order to join God where he's already at work around us.

# module six

## TIMES ARE CHANGING . . . SHOULD WE?

We've considered the importance of stretching beyond our normal bubble of comfort and security (everybody has one) in order to cross-culturally engage the next generation. Growth and transformation happen by purposely living *outside* our comfort zone. The fact that you've made it this far tells me you're willing to stretch yourself to do new things that will bring out new realities in your life and the lives of others.

The definition of *insanity* is doing the same thing over and over while expecting different results. Business as usual won't work when it comes to reaching the next generation. Waiting for them to come to us is not a strategy. Hoping that they "stick around" should they choose to come within the four walls of our building is not a strategy.

The COVID-19 crisis has forced all churches to redefine themselves as something more than groups who try to fill up a building or fill the calendar with events. This may be COVID-19's greatest gift to American Christianity. We have been forced to ask deeper questions about how lives are really shaped and what discipleship looks like when we cannot gather in large groups.

Can the gospel still go out and multiply in such an environment? I believe it can *explode* exponentially during these uncertain times. What can a virus teach us? The phrase "going viral" refers to the contagious ability of a virus to exponentially infect people who in turn accelerate infections in others. Humans are carriers of whatever is inside them. We're good at spreading what we have to others. Spreading whatever we have happens naturally and requires little effort. The hard part is *not* spreading what's inside us to others. Prior to COVID-19, most churches in America were not that contagious. If you measure church growth, it's clear that growing congregations were the exception, not the norm.

When it comes to making actual disciples (more than just filling a building), our task becomes even more clear. During the great commission, Jesus commanded us to go "and make disciples of all nations, baptizing them in the name of the Father and of the Son and of the Holy Spirit, teaching them to observe all that I have commanded you" (Matthew 28:19 ESV).

He did not say go and fill buildings.

He commands us to *go* (a command which often implies *leaving* the facility) and make disciples of all nations. Making disciples is harder than filling buildings. Building followers of Jesus is harder than beefing up followers on Instagram. Doing the hard work of discipleship is the way to change the world.

What if God allowed churches to be shut down in order to teach us how to really be contagious with the gospel? What if God has used COVID-19 to make believers sit outside the church building long enough to realize that Christ's command was always for us to *go* out in the first place? Don't get me wrong, human relationships and gathering is essential for well-being and spiritual growth. Nonetheless, these strange times we find ourselves in force us to rethink what it means to be followers of Jesus. Are we primarily attendees filling pews, buildings, and schedules, or contagious disciples who reproduce ourselves throughout the world? Filling up buildings was not a viral enough strategy when it comes to making actual contagious disciples.

Let's do a little thought experiment together. Imagine you are standing in front of two closed doors. You can only pick the contents that lie behind one. The first door opens. Sitting on the floor is a large briefcase full of $250,000 cash. Yours for the taking. You just have to make your selection.

But wait. What's behind door number two? I'm glad you asked! Door number two opens to reveal a penny sitting on top of an empty table. There is a note above the penny that reads, "This coin doubles every day for a month."

Which do you pick? You have ten seconds to make your selection? $250,000 cash or the magic doubling penny. Your call. Ready?

Now, what if I told you that when you start with $.01 and it doubles daily for 31 days (I picked a long month for dramatic effect!) you end up with . . . $10,737,418.20!!!! That is the power of multiplication. WOW!

Now, to really blow our minds, let's reflect on the power of *exponential* growth. To truly "go viral" each penny would *turn into* a penny that *also* reproduces itself over and over again. *That* is the potential of the church impacting the world! That is *exactly* how one Galilean carpenter (extra credit if you can name him!) and his band of renegade fishermen, tax collectors, tradesmen, and women of faith turned the world upside down . . . That is exactly how one human in Asia managed to infect 2,173,168 people in 191 of the world's 195 countries.

True discipleship is meant to go viral! In fact, it is *impossible* for an infected person to spend large amounts of time sharing life (eating, playing, working, worshipping, talking, shaking hands, hugging, traveling) in close proximity to other humans without them catching what you have. If someone has Coronavirus and spends time in close proximity to others, it is highly likely that people around them will catch what they have. When people catch Jesus from someone else, the person begins to exhibit *new* life-giving symptoms that lead to flourishing and wholeness rather than death.

Similarly, if someone shares life with you (eating, drinking, talking, laughing, hugging, shaking hands, playing, and working in your presence) and they *do not* end up with what you have, chances are . . . you are not carrying it in the first place!

## What Does This Mean for Our Day and Age?

The "Kerygma," or core gospel presentation, must get effectively translated into new cultures without changing its essence. Faithful Christians must discern how the unchanging truths of God get lived out across time and space.

Three primary commitments remain universal:

1. Kids still need Jesus.

2. Discipleship is the crux of the matter. (The "How" may change but "Who" and "Why" remain.)

3. Investing ourselves matters more now than ever.

"If you marry the spirit of your own generation, you will be a widow in the next . . . ." —Dean Inge

How do we faithfully engage culture while remaining true to the message of Jesus? This is the core question for caring adults who want to "get kids." When an individual, family, group, or organization talks about *change*, the natural response for all of us is to think about what it will *cost* us. We like the familiar – even if it is less than ideal – because at least we know what to expect!

But let me ask you a different question. What is the *cost* of *not* changing? To you? To your calling? To others? To the kingdom? Do you dare to let the Holy Spirit do a deep work of change in you through our time together? Having made it this far, I believe the change is already underway. So, here's your homework . . .

Here's a personal invitation to our Caring Adult Mastermind. Would you like to join me along with other like-minded leaders for an extraordinary retreat? If so, we would be honored to have you. Contact us for more details at courses.uyc.org/contact-us.

Or perhaps you'd like an even more personal approach. I offer one-on-one coaching and consulting for leaders like you that want to take their life and influence to the next level. Join me on the journey of significance. Learn more at courses.uyc.org/coaching.

Thank you for spending this time with me. I pray it is not the last time we interact. I look forward to being a conversation partner and companion on the journey of life with you. Stay in touch with me at courses.uyc.org/contact-us.


*Now may the Lord bless you and keep you. May He make His face shine on you and be gracious to you. May He turn His face toward you and give you His peace. In the name of the Father, and of the Son, and of the Holy Spirit. Amen.*

*God bless you! Until next time . . . Go in His peace.*

# YOU DID IT!

*Congratulations* on finishing this book on youth relationships. You're now better equipped to invest your life and engage the next generation. But don't stop here. There are many ways to continue growing. I have two additional books (and corresponding video courses):

- Church Leader Course
  (courses.uyc.org/Church-Leader)

- Student Leader Course
  (courses.uyc.org/Student-Leader)

My team and I are also available for elite coaching and consulting. As a graduate of this course, I am offering you a special rate for a limited time. Check your email from me for next steps.

I look forward to walking more closely with you through the next chapter of your life with God.

Your life is a gift to me and so many others!

Excited for your growth and impact,

Kate